Year after year, a maple tree changes from season to season.

In winter the tree is bare. It looks dead, but it is alive and well. Many things are happening.

Squirrels nap in
a cozy tree hole.

A little bird sits
on a branch and
calls its name:
Chicka-dee-dee-dee!

Look closely at this tree
branch. The bumps at the
tip are buds. They will
open into leaves when the
weather gets warmer.

As winter ends, nights are still cold, but days are getting warmer.

It is perfect weather for farmers to collect sugar maple sap.

The sap flows out of taps and into buckets.

The sap has no color until it is boiled. Then it becomes dark sweet maple syrup.

What a treat for pancakes and waffles!

Spring brings warmer weather.

The leaf buds open.

Soon the maple tree grows floppy green flower tassels.

Birds build nests on the branches.

Spring also brings rain showers.

The tree's roots
soak up water
and carry it to all
parts of the tree.

Sunshine helps the tree make sap, which feeds the tree.

Look at the veins in a leaf. Air, water, and sap all flow through them.

In summer the maple tree is covered with dark green leaves.

Fruit, called samaras, is growing on the tree. It makes a good meal for a chipmunk.

Even on a hot summer day, you can find a cool place to play under a maple tree.

In autumn the tree's
leaves turn bright colors.

As the leaves dry up, they change from green to yellow, red, and orange. Each day more and more leaves fall.

Autumn brings chilly days and nights.

Bugs crawl under the tree's bark where they will sleep through the cold weather.

Animals get ready for winter when food will be hard to find. Squirrels hide lots of nuts and seeds.

If you play in the leaves you'll hear crunch, scrunch, crunch! But don't worry about making noise. The maple tree won't wake up again until spring.